301 Ace-tastic Facts: Tennis Edition

M.K. Publishing House

Copyright © [2024] by [M.K. Publishing House]

All rights reserved.

No portion of this book may be reproduced in any form without written permission from the publisher or author, except as permitted by U.S. copyright law.

Contents

1. Grand Slam Tournaments — 1
2. Tennis Legends — 12
3. The Evolution of Tennis — 24
4. Tennis Court and Surfaces — 35
5. Amazing Records and Achievements — 46
6. Tennis Gear and Technology — 57
7. Fun Tennis Facts and Trivia — 68
8. Tennis Around the World — 79
9. Junior Tennis and Youth Stars — 89
10. Tennis for Everyone — 100

Chapter One

Grand Slam Tournaments

Facts about the four major tournaments (Australian Open, French Open, Wimbledon, and US Open) and their unique traditions.

1. The Australian Open used to be played on grass courts, just like Wimbledon! But in 1988, they changed to blue hard courts. The players really like these courts because they can see the bright yellow tennis balls better against the blue surface. The tournament happens in January when it's super hot in Australia – sometimes the temperature gets so high they have to close the roof!

2. At Wimbledon, all tennis players must wear completely white clothes – even their socks and shoes! This rule is super strict and started way back in the 1800s when people thought sweat stains on colored clothes looked yucky. Even famous players like Roger Federer and Serena Williams have to follow this rule, no matter how much they might want to wear colorful outfits!

3. The French Open is played on red clay courts, which aren't actually made of clay! They're made from crushed brick that's spread over the ground. When players slide on these courts, their white socks and shoes turn orange-red. The clay makes the tennis balls bounce higher and slower, which is why some players call it the trickiest tournament to win.

4. The US Open is known for being super noisy! Unlike the quiet atmosphere at Wimbledon, fans at the US Open love to cheer, clap, and make lots of noise between points. The tournament even has special night match-

es that feel like a big party, with music playing during breaks and colorful lights shining everywhere.

5. At the Australian Open, they have a special bird problem! Sometimes, flocks of seagulls like to land right on the tennis courts during matches. The tournament has to use specially trained birds of prey, like hawks, to scare away the seagulls. These guardian birds patrol the skies above the courts to keep the pesky seagulls away!

6. Wimbledon is crazy about strawberries and cream! Every year, fans eat about 27,000 kilograms of strawberries with fresh cream. That's the same weight as four big elephants! The strawberries are picked fresh every morning at 4:00 AM and delivered to the tournament before the matches start.

7. The French Open trophy is called "La Coupe des Mousquetaires" for men, named after the famous French tennis players known as "The Four Musketeers." These players were super popular in France during the

1920s and 1930s. The trophy is so heavy that some players struggle to lift it when they win!

8. The US Open was the first Grand Slam tournament to give equal prize money to men and women winners. This happened in 1973, and the tournament is really proud of this fact! They also were the first to use instant replay technology to check if balls were in or out.

9. At the Australian Open, players sometimes have to deal with super weird weather! One day it might be burning hot at 40°C (104°F), and the next day it could be raining with cold winds. Players have to be ready for anything, and sometimes matches get delayed because of extreme heat or rain.

10. Wimbledon has a very special royal connection! The Royal Family often comes to watch matches, and players have to bow or curtsy when passing the Royal Box. There's even a special Royal Box attendant who makes

sure everything is perfect for the royal visitors, including their favorite snacks and drinks!

11. The French Open ball kids have a special way of rolling tennis balls across the court! They have to crouch down low and roll the balls super fast along the ground, making them look like little ninjas darting around. They practice this move for months before the tournament starts.

12. The US Open has a super cool tradition of playing matches at night under bright lights! It was the first Grand Slam to do this, starting in 1975. The atmosphere is amazing, with the New York City skyline lit up in the background and fans staying up late to watch exciting tennis matches.

13. The Australian Open has special "Happy Slam" nickname because players love it so much! They get treated like movie stars, with fancy hotels, amazing restaurants, and even their own drivers. The tourna-

ment also has a beach-themed area where fans can watch matches while sitting in beach chairs!

14. At Wimbledon, there's a very important person called the "Chief Honorary Weatherman." This person's only job is to decide if it's going to rain and if they need to close the roof over Centre Court. They even use special weather balloons to help make these important decisions!

15. The French Open courts are swept in a special way between matches! The maintenance team uses big brushes to make special patterns in the clay, kind of like drawing in a zen garden. They have to be super careful to make sure the court is perfectly flat for the next match.

16. The US Open ball persons (that's what they call ball kids there) have to pass a super tough test to get their job! They need to be able to throw a tennis ball across the whole court without it bouncing, and they

have to be as quiet as mice while running around during matches.

17. The Australian Open has a huge party on the last Saturday night called the "Players' Party." All the tennis players dress up in fancy clothes and dance together, even if they lost their matches! They also have a special kids' tennis day where young fans can meet their favorite players.

18. Wimbledon has a special team of cats that live at the tennis club! Their job is to keep mice away from the grass courts. These cats are treated like royalty and even have their own special caretaker. They're not allowed on the courts during matches, but they patrol the grounds at night.

19. At the French Open, players often end up with red clay all over their clothes and shoes! The tournament has special washing machines that know exactly how to clean the red clay stains. Players sometimes go through

three or four outfit changes during a single match because of all the clay!

20. The US Open has a special "Food Village" that's like a mini food festival! Fans can try foods from all over the world while watching tennis. They even have a special tennis ball-shaped ice cream that turns your tongue blue, just like the color of the tennis courts!

21. The Australian Open has a funny rule about birds landing on the net during matches! If a bird lands on the net and the ball hits the net, players have to replay the point, even if the ball would have gone in! This rule was made after a famous match where a cockatoo caused chaos.

22. At Wimbledon, there's a special person whose job is to look after the grass on the tennis courts! They measure the grass every single day to make sure it's exactly 8 millimeters tall. If it's even a tiny bit too long or

too short, they have to fix it before any matches can be played.

23. The French Open has a secret underground tunnel system! Players use these tunnels to move between courts without getting stuck in crowds. The tunnels are painted with pictures of famous French tennis moments, and some players say it feels like being in a sports museum!

24. The US Open stadium has a special roof that can close in just 5 minutes and 20 seconds! That's about the same time it takes to microwave a bag of popcorn. The roof is so high that you could fit the Statue of Liberty inside the stadium (if you took her off her base)!

25. At the Australian Open, they have special "Cool Rooms" where players can go if they get too hot during matches! These rooms are kept at exactly 15°C (59°F) and have special ice vests that players can wear. Some players say it feels like walking into a freezer!

26. Wimbledon has official ball boys and girls (they call them BBGs) who train for six months before the tournament! They learn special hand signals and have to stand in a specific way called the "Wimbledon stance." They're not allowed to cheer or show any emotion during matches.

27. The French Open trophy for women is called "Coupe Suzanne Lenglen," named after a famous French tennis player who was known for drinking cognac between sets! She was also famous for wearing short skirts and playing with incredible style, which shocked people in the 1920s.

28. The US Open's court surface is made with 27 layers of different materials! It's like a giant sandwich made of concrete, rubber, and special paint. The top layer has tiny crystals in it that help absorb sweat and keep players from slipping during intense matches.

29. The Australian Open mascot is a really cool character called "Bounce!" It's a tennis ball with arms and legs who wears sunglasses and does funny dances between matches. Bounce has become so popular that they now sell stuffed toy versions at the tournament!

30. All four Grand Slam tournaments have their own special songs! Wimbledon has a traditional anthem, the French Open plays French classical music, the US Open rocks out to pop music, and the Australian Open has a special theme song that fans sing along to during breaks!

Chapter Two

Tennis Legends

Profiles of famous players like Roger Federer, Serena Williams, Rafael Nadal, and Billie Jean King, focusing on achievements and memorable moments.

1. Roger Federer was such a naughty ball boy when he was young! He would often get distracted watching matches instead of collecting tennis balls. Who knew this mischievous Swiss kid would grow up to win 20 Grand Slam tournaments? He became so famous for being graceful on court that people called him "The Swiss

Maestro" because he made tennis look like a beautiful dance!

2. Serena Williams started playing tennis when she was just four years old, using a racket that was almost as big as her! Her dad would push her tennis gear to practice in an old shopping cart. She became so strong that her serves could reach 128 miles per hour – that's faster than most cars are allowed to drive on the highway!

3. Rafael Nadal writes with his right hand but plays tennis with his left hand! His uncle Toni, who was his coach, thought it would give him an advantage in matches. Rafa is so superstitious that he never steps on court lines when walking onto the court, and his water bottles must be lined up perfectly with the labels facing the exact same way.

4. Billie Jean King won an amazing tennis match called "The Battle of the Sexes" in 1973. A male player named Bobby Riggs said girls couldn't play tennis as well as

boys, so Billie Jean proved him wrong in front of 90 million people watching on TV! She won easily and helped make sure women players got paid the same as men.

5. Novak Djokovic used to practice tennis in an empty swimming pool during wartime in Serbia! Can you imagine hitting tennis balls back and forth in a pool with no water? He also learned to ski before he could walk properly. Now he's won more Grand Slam tournaments than any other male player in tennis history!

6. Venus Williams is super tall – 6 feet 1 inch! When she was learning tennis, her dad would write positive messages on poster boards and hold them up during her practice. She became so good at serving that she hit the fastest serve ever recorded in women's tennis at Wimbledon – it was 129 miles per hour!

7. Andre Agassi hated tennis when he was young because his dad made him hit 2,500 tennis balls every

single day! His dad built a special machine called "the dragon" that would shoot balls at young Andre. Despite hating it at first, he grew to love the sport and became the first player to win all four Grand Slams on different court surfaces.

8. Martina Navratilova had a special friend at Wimbledon – a stray cat that wandered onto the tennis court during one of her matches! She ended up adopting the cat and named it "Fred." Martina was super fit and strong because she was one of the first tennis players to start lifting weights and exercising like other athletes.

9. Pete Sampras used to hit tennis balls against his family's garage door so much that his parents had to keep repainting it! His serve was so powerful and accurate that people nicknamed him "Pistol Pete." He won Wimbledon seven times but never won the French Open because he had trouble sliding on the clay courts.

10. John McEnroe was known for having a really bad temper on the tennis court! He would yell at the umpires and sometimes even break his tennis rackets. But he was also an amazing player who could hit the ball before it bounced, which was super tricky. He was so good at this that other players couldn't figure out how to beat him!

11. Chris Evert was nicknamed the "Ice Queen" because she never showed her feelings during matches! She would stay super calm even when playing really important points. She's the reason we call diamond bracelets "tennis bracelets" – because her bracelet broke during a match and she asked to stop playing until she found it!

12. Maria Sharapova was only 6 years old when she started playing tennis in Russia! She moved all the way to Florida to train when she was just 7 years old. She became famous for making loud grunting noises when hitting the ball – some people said it sounded like a baby

elephant! She won her first Wimbledon when she was just 17.

13. Arthur Ashe loved reading so much that he would bring books to read between matches! He was the first African American man to win Wimbledon, and he did it while wearing glasses. He was so smart that he graduated from college while being a professional tennis player – not many players did that back then!

14. Steffi Graf was so fast on the tennis court that people called her "Fraulein Forehand!" She won all four Grand Slam tournaments AND an Olympic gold medal in the same year – nobody else has ever done that! She was also super nice and would always write thank-you notes to the ball kids after her matches.

15. Andy Murray has two huge gold medals from winning tennis at the Olympics! When he was eight years old, he was in school during something very scary – but he survived by hiding under a desk. Now he's a hero in

Britain and was even given a special title by the Queen – they call him "Sir Andy Murray!"

16. Monica Seles was so good at tennis that she became world number one when she was only 17! She would grunt really loudly when hitting the ball, which some people didn't like, but it helped her hit the ball super hard. She loved playing video games between matches to help her relax and forget about feeling nervous.

17. Rod Laver was called "The Rocket" because he was super quick around the tennis court! He's the only tennis player to win all four Grand Slam tournaments twice in the same year – and he did it once playing with wooden rackets! His special shot was a powerful serve that curved like a banana.

18. Justine Henin was tiny compared to most tennis players – only 5 feet 5 inches tall! But she had the most beautiful one-handed backhand shot that people said looked like poetry in motion. She was so determined to

become a tennis star that she would practice hitting balls in any weather, even in the snow!

19. Boris Becker became the youngest ever Wimbledon champion when he won at just 17 years old! He would dive and jump around the court so much that people called him "Boom Boom Becker." He had bright red hair and would eat the same pasta meal before every match for good luck.

20. Margaret Court won more Grand Slam tournaments than any other tennis player ever – 64 in total! She was so tall and strong that other players were scared to play against her. She started playing tennis using a wooden racket that her parents cut down to make smaller for her little hands.

21. Björn Borg was called "Ice Borg" because he never seemed to get excited or angry during matches! He had long blonde hair and wore a headband that made him look like a Viking warrior. He was so popular that peo-

ple would scream and chase him around like he was a rock star!

22. Martina Hingis was named after Martina Navratilova and started playing tennis when she was two years old! She became the youngest Grand Slam champion ever when she won a doubles title at just 15 years old. She was so smart on the court that people called her "The Swiss Miss" because she always knew where to hit the ball.

23. Andy Roddick could serve the tennis ball faster than anyone else – his fastest serve was 155 miles per hour! That's as fast as some airplanes when they're taking off. He would practice his serve by trying to hit specific spots on the court, and he wouldn't stop until he hit them perfectly ten times in a row!

24. Tracy Austin was so young when she started winning tournaments that she still had braces on her teeth! She wore her hair in two braids tied with ribbons that

would bounce around when she played. She became the youngest US Open champion ever at 16 years old, and she did her homework between matches!

25. Mats Wilander won his first Grand Slam tournament when he was only 17, but he was so humble that he apologized to the player he beat! He would ride his bicycle to tennis matches to warm up, even at big tournaments. He was known for being so nice that other players voted him as the friendliest player on tour!

26. Kim Clijsters was so flexible that she could do the splits while hitting tennis balls! She was called "Super Girl" because she came back to win tournaments after having a baby – not many players had done that before. She was so nice to the ball kids that she would give them all chocolate after her matches.

27. Stan Wawrinka has a really cool tattoo on his arm that says "Ever tried. Ever failed. No matter. Try again. Fail again. Fail better." It helped him keep trying even

when tennis was really hard! He hits his backhand so hard that other players say it sounds like a cannon going off!

28. Caroline Wozniacki was so good at running that she could have been a marathon runner instead of a tennis player! She once ran a whole marathon after playing in a tennis tournament. She would practice tennis while wearing a mask that made it harder to breathe, to help her get super fit!

29. Gustavo Kuerten drew hearts on the clay court when he won matches! The crowds loved him so much they called him "Guga." He used to practice tennis using brooms instead of rackets when he was little because tennis equipment was too expensive. He became so good at playing on clay courts that he won three French Open titles!

30. Li Na was the first player from Asia to win a Grand Slam tournament! She was so funny in her speeches

after matches that people would laugh until their stomachs hurt. She started playing tennis because her coach told her she could eat as much ice cream as she wanted if she won – and she really loved ice cream!

Chapter Three

The Evolution of Tennis

How tennis started and changed over the years, from medieval France to modern-day global tournaments.

1. Tennis actually started as a game where people hit balls with their hands! In medieval France, monks would play this game in their monasteries during religious ceremonies. They would yell "Tenez!" (which means "take this!" in French) when hitting the ball, and that's how we got the word "tennis!" They played in these big stone courtyards for fun.

2. The first tennis rackets weren't made of metal or plastic – they were just people's hands in a leather glove! Lat-

er, they started using wooden paddles that looked like small canoe paddles. Some rich people would decorate their paddles with pretty paintings and gold designs. The leather gloves got thicker and thicker until someone thought of making a racket!

3. King Henry VIII of England was a huge tennis fan! He built a special tennis court at Hampton Court Palace that you can still visit today. He would get super angry if he lost a game and sometimes throw big tantrums. The king was actually playing tennis when he heard that his second wife was going to be arrested – talk about bad timing!

4. The first Wimbledon tournament in 1877 had some pretty funny rules! Players had to wear special shoes so they wouldn't hurt the grass, and men had to play wearing long pants and long-sleeved shirts. The prize for winning was only £12 - that's about as much as a video game costs today! Only 22 players entered the first tournament.

5. Tennis balls used to be white! They changed to bright yellow-green in 1972 because this color was easier to see on TV. The first tennis balls were made of leather stuffed with hair or wool. Some fancy ones were even made with human hair inside! Today's tennis balls are made of rubber covered with fuzzy felt.

6. The tennis scoring system (15, 30, 40, game) comes from medieval France too! They used a clock face to keep score, moving the hand a quarter way around for each point. That's why the first point is 15, the second is 30, and the third was supposed to be 45 but got shortened to 40 over time!

7. In the early days of tennis, some courts were shaped like an hourglass! The court was wider at the baselines and narrower in the middle, kind of like a bow tie. People thought this made the game more interesting, but players kept tripping over the lines, so they changed it to the rectangle shape we use today.

8. The first tennis players didn't run around during points – they stayed in one spot! This was because they wore fancy, heavy clothes and didn't want to get sweaty. They would just stand still and hit the ball back and forth until someone missed. Imagine playing tennis without moving your feet!

9. Women weren't allowed to play at Wimbledon until 1884, seven years after the men started! They had to play wearing long dresses that went all the way to their ankles, big hats, and tight corsets. Some brave women started wearing shorter skirts in the 1920s, which caused a big scandal!

10. Before tennis nets, they used to stretch a rope across the court! Players would have to hit the ball over the rope, and sometimes it would sag in the middle. Later, they added a strip of cloth hanging from the rope to make it easier to see. The first proper tennis nets were made from fishing nets!

11. The first tennis rackets were shaped like the letter P! They had a long handle and a small, round hitting area. They were made of solid wood and were so heavy that players could only use them for a short time before their arms got tired. Some rackets even had special compartments to hold snacks!

12. In the early 1900s, tennis players would carry their rackets in fancy wooden boxes! These boxes had special compartments for spare strings, balls, and even a little mirror to check their appearance. Some players would decorate their boxes with their initials made from gold or silver!

13. The longest tennis match ever played lasted for 11 hours and 5 minutes! It was played at Wimbledon in 2010 between John Isner and Nicolas Mahut. The match was so long that they had to play for three days because it kept getting too dark to continue. The scoreboard even broke because it wasn't designed for such high numbers!

14. Tennis used to be played on croquet lawns! That's why many old tennis clubs have the word "lawn" in their names. The grass had to be cut super short with special scissors to make it flat enough for tennis balls to bounce properly. Sometimes sheep would graze on the courts to keep the grass short!

15. The first tennis tournaments gave out really strange prizes! Winners might get a silver butter dish, a golden pineapple, or even a live sheep! At one tournament, the prize was a special tennis racket made entirely of chocolate. The winner couldn't even use it because it would melt in the sun!

16. Tennis players didn't always wear special tennis shoes! In the early days, they played in their regular leather shoes, which left big marks on the courts. Then someone invented special shoes with rubber soles that wouldn't damage the grass. These were called "plimsolls" and had funny little patterns on the bottom.

17. Before electronic scoreboards, they used to have kids sitting next to the courts holding up big number cards! These kids had to change the cards after every point, and sometimes they would get so excited watching the match that they'd forget to change the score. Some tournaments used pigeons to deliver score updates to the newspapers!

18. The first tennis serve was actually underhand! Players thought it was more polite to serve the ball gently underhand rather than smashing it overhand. When some players started serving overhand, people thought it was really rude and unfair. Now almost everyone serves overhand, and it's totally normal!

19. Tennis players used to wear their regular street clothes to play! Men would play in suits and ties, and women wore their everyday long dresses. They would even wear fancy hats while playing. On really hot days, players would just take off their jacket but keep their tie on – how uncomfortable!

20. The first tennis umpires sat in regular chairs on the ground! The tall umpire chairs we see today weren't invented until someone realized the umpires couldn't see the lines properly from ground level. The first tall chairs were actually old lifeguard chairs borrowed from the beach!

21. In the early days of tennis, players had to retrieve their own balls! There were no ball boys or ball girls to help them. Rich people would hire servants to stand around the court and collect balls for them. Sometimes they even used trained dogs to fetch the balls – imagine that at Wimbledon today!

22. The first tennis courts in America were built in people's backyards! Rich families would invite their friends over for "garden parties" where they would play tennis and have tea. Some people even built indoor tennis courts in their houses so they could play when it was raining or snowing outside.

23. Tennis racket strings used to be made from sheep intestines! These strings were called "natural gut" and were actually really good for playing tennis. They were expensive and would break easily in the rain. Today, most players use strings made from special plastic materials, but some still prefer the old-fashioned gut strings!

24. The first tennis tournaments didn't have any rules about making noise! Players would chat with their friends, laugh, and even sing while playing. At one tournament, a player brought his pet parrot that would squawk every time he won a point. Now players have to be quiet during points!

25. Tennis players didn't always change ends of the court during matches! They would stay on the same side the whole time, which wasn't fair if it was windy or sunny on one side. Someone finally suggested switching sides to make it more fair, and everyone thought it was such a good idea that it became a rule!

26. The first tennis line judges were volunteers from the audience! Tournament organizers would ask people watching the matches if they wanted to help judge the lines. Sometimes they would fall asleep during boring matches or argue with each other about whether balls were in or out!

27. Tennis used to be played all year round on the same type of court! Now we have different surfaces like grass, clay, and hard courts, but back then it was usually just grass. The first clay courts were made by accident when someone spilled crushed brick on a grass court and noticed the balls bounced differently!

28. The first tennis tournaments didn't have any prize money! Players competed for trophies, medals, or just for fun. Some tournaments would give out strange prizes like cases of champagne or fruit baskets. The first professional tennis players were actually teaching pros who gave lessons to rich people.

29. Tennis matches didn't always have tie-breakers! Games could go on forever until someone won by two clear games. One set at Wimbledon in 1969 lasted for 112 games! People got tired of matches taking so long, so they invented the tie-breaker in 1971 to make games end faster.

30. The earliest tennis courts had different shapes and sizes! Some were really long and narrow, while others were short and wide. It wasn't until 1875 that someone decided all tennis courts should be the same size. They measured out the perfect court size using a piece of string and some wooden stakes!

Chapter Four

Tennis Court and Surfaces

Explore the different court surfaces (clay, grass, hard court) and how they affect the game and players' styles.

1. Did you know tennis courts come in different colors? Hard courts can be blue, green, or even purple! The US Open changed their courts from green to blue in 2006 so that people could see the yellow tennis balls better on TV. Players say the bright blue courts make them feel like they're playing on top of a swimming pool!

2. Clay courts are actually made from crushed brick, not real clay! The tiny brick pieces get everywhere - in players' socks, shoes, and clothes. After every match, players'

white socks turn orange-red! The courts need special care, like being watered and swept with big brushes to keep the surface smooth and even.

3. Grass courts are like playing tennis on your backyard lawn, but super fancy! The grass at Wimbledon is cut to exactly 8 millimeters tall - about as tall as a small paper clip standing up. They have special lawn mowers that cut the grass the same way every day, and they even use vacuum cleaners to clean the courts!

4. Hard courts are like playing tennis on a giant sandwich! They're made of many layers - concrete on the bottom, then special rubber and acrylic materials on top. The top layer has tiny bits of sand mixed in to help players grip the court with their shoes. It's kind of like having super tiny skateboard grip tape under your feet!

5. Clay courts make tennis balls bounce higher and slower! This is why some players look like they're dancing on clay - they have to slide around to reach the

high-bouncing balls. Rafael Nadal loves clay courts so much that people call him the "King of Clay." He's won the French Open (played on clay) 14 times!

6. The grass at Wimbledon has a special rule - no pets allowed! This is because they don't want any animals digging holes or leaving marks on the perfect grass. They do make one exception though - they have special hawks that fly around to scare away pigeons that might try to land on the courts!

7. Hard courts can get super hot in the sun! Sometimes the surface temperature can reach 120°F (that's hotter than a hot bath!). Players have to wear special shoes that don't melt, and sometimes they put ice towels around their necks to stay cool. Some tournaments even have rules about taking breaks when it's too hot!

8. Clay courts have special white lines that are actually tape! Unlike other courts where the lines are painted, clay court lines are stuck down with special tape. After

every point, players can see their shoe marks in the clay, which helps the umpire see if balls were in or out - it's like having instant replay in the dirt!

9. Grass courts are the trickiest to take care of! The groundskeepers at Wimbledon have to check the grass for diseases, water it just the right amount, and even cover it up when birds fly overhead (because bird poop can damage the grass!). They also have to pray it doesn't rain too much, or the grass gets slippery!

10. Hard courts are the most common type in the world because they're the easiest to maintain! You don't have to water them like clay courts or mow them like grass courts. They're also great for playing in any weather - rain dries quickly on hard courts, and they don't get muddy or slippery like other surfaces.

11. Clay courts need a special way of sweeping between points! Players drag big brushes in special patterns to smooth out their footprints. It looks like they're draw-

ing giant pictures on the court! Some players are very particular about how the court is swept and will even do it themselves during matches.

12. The grass at Wimbledon gets replanted every year! After the tournament ends, they dig up all the old grass and plant new grass seeds. It takes 15 months to grow the perfect grass court surface. The grass has to be a special type that's strong enough for tennis but soft enough to not hurt players when they fall.

13. Indoor hard courts feel different from outdoor ones! The walls and roof of indoor courts can make tennis balls bounce differently, and there's no sun or wind to deal with. Some players say it feels like playing tennis in a giant shoebox! The lights on the ceiling can sometimes make it tricky to see high balls.

14. Clay courts make a special sound when players slide on them! It's like a squeaky-scratchy noise that tells you someone is running and sliding to hit the ball. Some

players practice their sliding sounds just as much as their tennis shots! The best clay court players can slide several feet without falling.

15. Grass courts have a special smell! When the grass gets cut, it releases a fresh, sweet smell that tennis players say reminds them of summer. The groundskeepers cut the grass every morning before matches start, so the courts always smell like freshly mowed lawn. Some players say they can tell how fast the court will be by its smell!

16. Different colored hard courts affect how fast the ball seems to move! On blue courts, the yellow ball looks like it's moving slower because blue and yellow are contrasting colors. On green courts, the ball can be harder to see because green and yellow are similar colors. That's why most tournaments now use blue courts!

17. Clay courts come in two colors - red and green! Most clay courts are red, but some are made with green clay (like the ones they used to have at the US Open).

The green clay is actually crushed basalt rock instead of brick. Players say the green clay is faster than the red clay, but it's harder to see the ball marks.

18. Grass courts have different "wear spots" where the grass gets worn away during matches! Near the baseline (where players stand to serve), the grass often disappears by the end of the tournament because so many players have run over it. These spots can make the ball bounce differently, like a mini-surprise for players!

19. Hard courts can be painted with fun designs! Some courts have special artwork painted on them, like giant company logos or cool patterns. In parks, you might see hard courts with other game lines painted on them too, like for basketball or hopscotch. It's like having multiple playgrounds in one!

20. Clay courts need special shoes! Players wear shoes with zigzag patterns on the bottom that help them slide better. These shoes would be too slippery for other

court types, but on clay, they help players move like ice skaters! You can always tell a clay court player by the orange dust on their shoes.

21. The grass at Wimbledon has its own doctor! Well, not a real doctor, but a special scientist who checks the grass every day to make sure it's healthy. They use special machines to measure how bouncy the grass is and even check each blade of grass to make sure it's the right type of grass plant!

22. Hard courts can make different sounds depending on how they're built! Some courts make a hollow sound when the ball bounces, while others make a sharp, crisp sound. Players often bounce the ball before serving to test how the court sounds - it's like they're playing a giant drum!

23. Clay courts are great for seeing where the ball landed! When a ball hits the clay, it leaves a mark that everyone can see. This helps umpires make decisions about

whether balls were in or out. Players often point to these marks when they disagree with a call - it's like having a dirt detective solve tennis mysteries!

24. Some grass courts have underground robots! At some fancy tennis clubs, they use robot lawn mowers that come out at night to cut the grass. These robots follow special patterns and never get tired. They're like little tennis court ninjas that work while everyone is sleeping!

25. Hard courts can have heating systems under them! In cold places, some courts have pipes under the surface that warm up the court. This helps melt snow and ice in winter so people can play tennis all year round. It's like having a giant heating pad under the tennis court!

26. Clay courts need to be "healed" after every match! The groundskeepers use special tools to fix all the spots where players have slid and left marks. They also water the courts to keep the clay from turning into dust. It's

like giving the court a spa treatment after a long day of tennis!

27. Grass courts sometimes have small bumps called "bobbles"! These happen when the grass gets worn down unevenly, making the ball bounce in funny ways. Players have to watch out for these bobbles, especially in the later days of tournaments when the grass is more worn out. It's like playing tennis on a very gentle roller-coaster!

28. Hard courts can have different speeds! Tournament organizers can make hard courts faster or slower by changing how much sand they mix into the top layer. Fast courts are great for big servers, while slower courts are better for players who like long rallies. It's like having a volume control for the court's speed!

29. Some clay courts have special heating systems too! These help dry the courts faster after rain and prevent them from freezing in cold weather. The heat makes the

clay turn different shades of red - lighter when it's warm and darker when it's cool. It's like having a mood ring tennis court!

30. Grass courts used to have lumps and bumps on purpose! In the early days of tennis, courts were uneven to make the game more interesting. Players had to guess how the ball would bounce off these bumps. Now, tennis courts are made as flat as possible - imagine trying to play tennis on a bumpy court today!

Chapter Five

Amazing Records and Achievements

Impressive records, like longest matches, highest number of Grand Slam titles, and fastest serves.

1. The longest tennis match ever was like watching three whole movies back-to-back! John Isner and Nicolas Mahut played for 11 hours and 5 minutes at Wimbledon in 2010. They played for three whole days because it kept getting too dark to continue. The final score was so long that the scoreboard broke - it couldn't show such big numbers!

2. The fastest tennis serve ever was hit by Sam Groth at 163.7 miles per hour! That's faster than some racing cars! If you blinked, you would miss the ball completely. Most commercial airplanes take off at about this speed. The serve was so fast that the player returning it barely saw the ball before it went past them!

3. Novak Djokovic holds the record for being ranked World No. 1 for the most weeks - over 400 weeks! That's almost 8 years of being the best tennis player in the world. Imagine being the best at something for that long! He's held the top spot for so long that some players who are now professionals were just little kids when he first became No. 1.

4. Margaret Court won 64 Grand Slam titles when you count singles, doubles, and mixed doubles! That's more than any other tennis player in history. She won so many trophies that she needed a special room just to keep them all. She won her first Grand Slam when she was just 17 and kept winning for 15 more years!

5. Venus Williams holds the record for the fastest serve in women's tennis at 129 miles per hour! That's about as fast as a cheetah can run. She hit this super-speed serve at Wimbledon, and it made a sound like a thunderclap when it hit the court. Most cars aren't even allowed to drive that fast on highways!

6. The longest tennis point ever lasted 29 minutes! Vicki Nelson and Jean Hepner hit the ball back and forth 643 times in one point at a tournament in 1984. That's like doing jumping jacks for half an hour straight! The players were so tired after this point that they could barely continue the match.

7. Rafael Nadal has won the French Open 14 times - more than anyone has won any other tournament! He's so good on clay courts that people call him the "King of Clay." He's won so many times that they put a statue of him outside the stadium. That's like winning the biggest race in your school every year for 14 years!

8. Roger Federer once won 237 weeks in a row as World No. 1! That's more than 4 years of being the best tennis player on Earth without anyone beating him to the top spot. During this time, he won so many matches that some people thought he was unbeatable. He was ranked No. 1 for so long that people started calling the top spot "Federer's spot"!

9. Serena Williams has won 23 Grand Slam singles titles - more than any other player in the modern era! She won her first one when she was just 17 years old and her last one when she was pregnant! That's like winning the biggest prize in your favorite video game 23 different times, each time getting harder than the last.

10. The shortest tennis match ever was only 20 minutes long! Jack Harper beat J. Sandiford 6-0, 6-0 at Wimbledon in 1946. That's shorter than most TV shows! The match was so quick that some spectators missed it because they were still buying their snacks when it ended.

11. Steffi Graf is the only tennis player to win all four Grand Slams AND an Olympic gold medal in the same year! This happened in 1988, and people called it the "Golden Slam." It's like winning five super-hard video game levels all in a row without making any mistakes! Nobody else has ever done this in singles tennis.

12. The longest rally in a professional tennis match had 643 hits over the net! The players must have felt like their arms were made of jelly afterward. Some people who were watching the match said they got dizzy just from moving their heads back and forth to follow the ball!

13. Martina Navratilova won an amazing 167 tennis tournaments in her career! That's like having enough trophies to give one to every kid in two whole elementary schools. She played professional tennis for 31 years - longer than most kids have been alive! She won her last tournament when she was 49 years old.

14. The youngest player to ever win a professional tennis match was Michael Chang at 15 years and 6 months old! He was still in high school when he started beating adult professional players. He had to get permission from his teachers to miss school to play in tournaments!

15. John Isner served 113 aces (serves that weren't returned) in one match! That's more aces than there are cards in two decks of playing cards. His opponent must have felt like he was trying to catch lightning bolts! The match was so long that they had to change the tennis balls 16 times.

16. Venus and Serena Williams have played against each other 31 times in professional matches! That's more matches than most brothers and sisters play in their whole lives. They've played each other in 9 Grand Slam finals - imagine competing for the biggest prize in tennis against your own sister!

17. Roger Federer went 10 years without missing a Grand Slam tournament! From 2000 to 2016, he played in 65 Grand Slams in a row. That's like never missing a single day of school for 10 years straight! He traveled around the world four times each year to play in these tournaments.

18. The longest tennis game ever played went to 70-68 in the fifth set! That's more points than most players score in an entire tournament. The players served over 200 aces between them, and both players broke records for the most serves in a match. They played for so long that both players got blisters on their feet!

19. Esther Vergeer won 470 wheelchair tennis matches in a row! She didn't lose a single match for 10 years straight. That's like winning every game you play from second grade all the way through middle school! She was so good that she won all four Paralympic gold medals in singles tennis.

20. Pete Sampras served 1,011 aces in one year! That's almost three aces every day for a whole year. His serve was so powerful that some players would step way back behind the baseline just to have a chance at returning it. People called him "Pistol Pete" because his serves were as fast as bullets!

21. The Bryan brothers won 16 Grand Slam doubles titles together! Being twins, they could almost read each other's minds on the court. They played together for 26 years - longer than any other doubles team in history. They even had special celebration moves they would do after winning matches!

22. Andre Agassi is the only male player to win all four Grand Slams on three different surfaces! He won on grass, clay, and hard courts. That's like being great at playing your favorite game on three completely different types of game consoles! He's also the only player to win all four Grand Slams while wearing a wig.

23. Billie Jean King won 20 Wimbledon titles when you count singles, doubles, and mixed doubles! She won so many times that they named a huge tennis center in New York after her. She was so popular that she even played a famous match called "The Battle of the Sexes" that was watched by 90 million people on TV!

24. Novak Djokovic has won more prize money than any other tennis player in history! He's won over $150 million just from playing tennis - that's more money than most people earn in their whole lives! He could buy about 30 million tennis balls with all that money (but he probably doesn't need that many!).

25. Monica Seles won eight Grand Slam titles before she turned 20! That's like becoming a champion while you're still a teenager. She was so young when she started winning that some of her opponents were more than twice her age! She hit the ball with both hands on both sides, which was very unusual.

26. Ivo Karlovic hit 78 aces in a single match at Wimbledon! That's more aces than there are keys on a piano. He's so tall (6 feet 11 inches) that when he serves, it's like the ball is coming down from a second-story window! Some players said trying to return his serve was like trying to catch raindrops.

27. Lleyton Hewitt became the youngest male player to be ranked World No. 1 at age 20! He was so young that he still had his learner's permit when he first became the best tennis player in the world. Some of the ball kids at his matches were only a few years younger than him!

28. The Williams sisters have won 14 Grand Slam doubles titles together! They're so good as a team that they've never lost a Grand Slam doubles final when playing together. That's like having a perfect score on every big test you take with your best friend! They even won three Olympic gold medals playing doubles together.

29. Rafael Nadal once won 81 matches in a row on clay courts! That's like winning every game you play for an entire school year. He was so good on clay that some players said it felt like he had super powers when playing on the red surface. His winning streak lasted for 145 days!

30. Jimmy Connors played in 1,557 professional tennis matches in his career! That's more matches than there are days in four years. He played so many matches that he wore out over 300 tennis rackets during his career. Some people calculated that he ran about 10,000 miles just during his matches - that's like running across the United States three times!

Chapter Six

Tennis Gear and Technology

From wooden rackets to high-tech gear, learn how equipment has evolved to enhance the game.

1. The first tennis rackets were made of wood and looked like tiny canoe paddles! They were super heavy - about as heavy as a jug of milk. Players had to have really strong arms to swing them. These old wooden rackets would sometimes crack or break during matches, especially on cold days. Today's rackets are so light they feel like toys compared to those old ones!

2. Tennis balls used to be white, but they changed to bright yellow-green in 1972! This happened because people watching tennis on TV couldn't see the white balls very well. The first tennis balls were made of leather and stuffed with wool or hair. Today's tennis balls are filled with pressurized air and covered in fuzzy felt - like tiny green fuzzy planets!

3. Modern tennis strings are super amazing! They can be made from cow intestines (called natural gut), special plastics, or even materials used in bulletproof vests. The strings are so strong that they can hold weight equal to a small car, but they're as thin as spaghetti! Players can change how tight they want their strings, like tuning a guitar.

4. Tennis shoes have changed so much! The first tennis players wore normal leather shoes that left black marks on the courts. Now, tennis shoes are like tiny spaceships for your feet - they have special soles that help players stop and start quickly, cushions for jumping, and mate-

rials that let your feet breathe. Some even have computers inside to track movement!

5. Modern tennis rackets have holes in the frame that make them swish through the air faster! Scientists discovered that putting holes in the sides of the racket frame reduces air resistance, just like in race cars. These holes also make the racket lighter without making it weaker. It's like Swiss cheese, but for tennis!

6. Players used to fix their own broken strings during matches with spare pieces of string! Now they have special machines that can string a racket perfectly in just 20 minutes. These machines use computers to make sure every string has exactly the same tension - tighter than a trampoline but not so tight that it breaks!

7. Tennis clothes have become like superhero suits! They're made from special materials that help sweat evaporate quickly and keep players cool. Some tennis clothes even have tiny holes in the fabric that are smaller

than raindrops but big enough to let air flow through. It's like wearing an air conditioner!

8. The first tennis nets were just ropes stretched across the court! Now, tennis nets are made from super-strong materials that can handle balls hitting them at over 100 miles per hour. The net posts even have special measuring sticks inside them to make sure the net is exactly the right height - 3 feet tall in the middle!

9. Modern tennis rackets have sweet spots bigger than your hand! The sweet spot is the best place to hit the ball on your racket. Old wooden rackets had sweet spots the size of a quarter. Today's rackets use science to make this spot much bigger, which helps players hit better shots. It's like having a magic wand that makes tennis easier!

10. Tennis balls are kept in pressurized cans to keep them bouncy! When you open a new can of tennis balls, the "pop" sound is air rushing in. Tournament players use new balls every few games because the balls lose their

bounce, like a balloon slowly losing air. Some tournaments use over 50,000 tennis balls!

11. The grip on tennis rackets used to be just leather wrapped around wood! Now, grips are made from special materials that stay dry even when your hands are sweaty. Some grips can even change color when they get too wet, telling players it's time to change them. It's like having a mood ring on your racket!

12. Tennis players now use computers to analyze their serves! Special cameras can track how fast the ball is spinning, where it bounces, and even what shape it makes in the air. This helps players improve their technique, like having a robot coach that can see things human eyes can't see.

13. Some tennis rackets now have sensors built into the handle! These sensors can tell players how hard they're hitting the ball, where on the racket they're hitting it, and even how much spin they're putting on the ball.

The information goes straight to a phone app - it's like having a tiny tennis teacher inside your racket!

14. Tennis courts can now tell if a ball is in or out by themselves! They use special cameras and computers that can track the ball faster than human eyes. This system is called "Hawk-Eye" and can show exactly where the ball landed, even if it was moving super fast. It's like having robot line judges!

15. Modern tennis bags are like portable locker rooms! They have special compartments that keep rackets at the right temperature, pockets that keep drinks cold, and even spaces for computers and phones. Some bags can carry up to 12 rackets! They're like Mary Poppins' magical bag, but for tennis stuff.

16. The strings in tennis rackets can now tell players if they're hitting too hard or too soft! Special electronic strings change color or send signals to a phone when the ball is hit. This helps players learn the perfect amount of

power to use, like having a traffic light for your tennis shots.

17. Tennis clothes now have built-in sunscreen! The fabric is made with tiny particles that block harmful sun rays. Some clothes even have special cooling zones in places where players get hottest, like under their arms and on their backs. It's like wearing a shield against the sun!

18. Modern tennis courts can change color depending on the weather! Some courts have special paint that gets lighter when it's hot and darker when it's cool. This helps players see the ball better and keeps the court from getting too hot. It's like having a giant mood ring to play tennis on!

19. Tennis rackets used to be strung with animal gut - like from sheep or cows! Now there are over 200 different types of strings made from materials scientists created in laboratories. Some strings are even made from

fishing line material! Players can choose strings that help them hit harder or with more spin.

20. Ball machines have become like tennis robots! Modern machines can be controlled by phone apps and can shoot balls in any pattern you want. They can even remember your favorite practice routines and make the balls spin different ways. It's like having a tireless practice partner that never gets tired!

21. Some tennis courts now have special bubble domes that go over them! These bubbles are held up by air pressure and protect players from rain and snow. They're like giant umbrellas that let you play tennis all year round, even when it's storming outside!

22. Tennis players now use special watches that track how far they run during matches! These watches can also measure how hard their heart is beating and how tired they're getting. Some can even predict when a play-

er needs to drink water or eat a snack - like having a tiny doctor on your wrist!

23. Modern tennis balls are made by machines that can produce 20,000 balls every day! Each ball has to bounce to exactly the same height when dropped from the same spot. The machines even check to make sure every ball weighs the same amount - they're pickier than your mom checking your homework!

24. Some tennis rackets now have lights built into them! These lights show players where to hit the ball for different shots. It's like having a GPS for your tennis shots! The lights can also show when you're swinging the racket too fast or too slow, like a traffic light for your tennis swing.

25. Tennis players now use special cooling vests between matches! These vests have pockets filled with ice or special cooling gel that helps players stay cool in hot weath-

er. It's like wearing a portable refrigerator! Some vests can stay cool for up to two hours.

26. Modern tennis courts can collect rainwater under the surface! This water is stored in tanks and used to water the court when it gets too dry. Some courts even have heating systems under them to dry them quickly after rain - like having a giant hair dryer built into the ground!

27. Tennis rackets are now tested in wind tunnels - just like airplanes! Scientists use these tests to make rackets that can cut through the air faster and with less effort. They can see how air moves around the racket using special smoke and cameras - it's like doing science experiments with tennis equipment!

28. Some tennis nets now have sensors that can tell if a serve touches the net! When this happens, it makes a sound to let everyone know there was a "let" serve. It's much more accurate than the old way of having some-

one touch the net with their hand to feel for vibrations - like having robot fingers on the net!

29. Tennis players can now get custom-made rackets using 3D printers! These printers can make racket handles that fit a player's hand perfectly, like making a glove that fits only you. Some players even have their names or lucky numbers printed right into the racket frame!

30. The latest tennis shoes have GPS trackers built into them! These can show coaches exactly how their players move around the court during matches. The shoes can even measure how high players jump and how quickly they change direction - it's like having a tiny sports scientist in your shoes!

Chapter Seven

Fun Tennis Facts and Trivia

Quirky, lesser-known facts about the sport, like odd rules, strange superstitions, and fun stats.

1. At Wimbledon, players used to bow or curtsy to pigeons! In the early days, carrier pigeons were used to send match scores to newspapers. The players would show respect to these "official birds" when they flew by. Now players only bow to the Royal Family in the special Royal Box - much fancier than bowing to birds!

2. Tennis players have super weird superstitions! Rafael Nadal must have his water bottles lined up perfectly, with the labels facing the court. He also never steps on the lines when walking onto the court. It's like playing "don't step on the cracks" but in a professional tennis match!

3. The first tennis players used to yell "Tenez!" (which means "take this!" in French) when serving the ball. That's how we got the word "tennis"! Imagine if we still did that today - matches would sound like a bunch of people shouting French words back and forth across the court!

4. Some tennis players bounce the ball exactly the same number of times before every serve - it's like their lucky number! Novak Djokovic bounces the ball up to 28 times before important serves. That's a lot of bouncing! Some fans count along with him, like it's a very slow game of basketball.

5. A tennis ball at Wimbledon must be exactly this color: Pantone 729 C! They're so picky about the color that they test balls with a special machine. If a ball is even a tiny bit too light or dark green, it's not allowed in matches. It's like having a very strict crayon inspector!

6. Tennis players used to drink milk and eat sandwiches during match breaks! Now they have special sports drinks and energy bars, but in the old days, you might see players having a picnic between sets. One player even drank coffee and ate chocolate cake during matches - not the best tennis snack!

7. There's a special tennis tournament just for mice in Thailand! The mice don't actually play tennis (that would be silly!), but they race around a tiny tennis court chasing a ball. The winning mouse gets a tiny trophy and lots of cheese. It's like having a tennis-themed hamster race!

8. Some tennis players talk to their tennis balls! They believe that talking nicely to the ball will make it go where they want it to. Andre Agassi used to whisper to his tennis balls before important serves. It's like having a tiny, round, fuzzy friend that helps you win matches!

9. The longest tennis match ever was so long that the scoreboard broke! It couldn't show numbers that big. The match lasted 11 hours and 5 minutes, and they had to play for three days because it kept getting too dark. The players were so tired they could barely lift their arms to shake hands at the end!

10. Tennis players aren't allowed to use the bathroom whenever they want during matches! They get special "bathroom breaks" and can only go at certain times. If they really need to go at the wrong time, too bad - they have to hold it! It's like being in school when the teacher says "not during class time."

11. Some tennis courts have had really weird colors! There have been pink courts, black courts, and even a blue clay court that players said felt like playing on ice. Most players didn't like the blue clay because they kept slipping and sliding around like penguins on ice!

12. In the early days of tennis, some players would carry snacks in their racket handles! The old wooden rackets had hollow handles where players could store cookies or candy. Imagine reaching into your tennis racket for a snack during a match - it's like having a secret candy drawer in your sports equipment!

13. There used to be a rule that ball boys and girls had to be exactly the same height! They thought it looked neater when all the kids were lined up at the same height. Now they care more about how fast you can run and catch balls than how tall you are - which makes much more sense!

14. Some tennis players have lucky underwear they wear for important matches! They think wearing the same pair brings good luck (hopefully after washing them!). One player wore the same pair of socks for a whole tournament because he thought they were lucky - pretty stinky by the end!

15. Tennis players used to wear long pants and dresses with lots of petticoats! Imagine trying to run and hit tennis balls while wearing clothes that look like you're going to a fancy party. Players would get so tangled up in their clothes that they sometimes tripped and fell!

16. The tennis scoring system (15, 30, 40, game) comes from medieval clock faces! Each point moved the clock hand a quarter way around. That's why the first point is 15 and the second is 30. The third point was supposed to be 45 but got shortened to 40 because players got tired of saying such big numbers!

17. Some tennis players have given their rackets names! Roger Federer named his racket "Wilson" (like in the movie Castaway), and one player called his racket "Betty." It's like having a pet that helps you win tennis matches! Some players even talk to their rackets when they're playing badly.

18. There's a special person at Wimbledon whose only job is to check if birds might poop on the courts! They use hawks to scare away pigeons that might make a mess on the perfect grass courts. The hawk's name is Rufus, and he has his own security pass - he's like a bird bouncer!

19. Tennis players have done some really silly victory dances! One player did the worm dance on the court after winning, another did cartwheels, and some players even climb up to hug their family in the stands. It's like having a dance party right after winning a match!

20. Some tennis tournaments have had really weird prizes! Players have won live animals (like sheep or chickens), fruit baskets, and even their weight in olive oil. Imagine winning a tennis match and getting a sheep as your prize - what would you do with it?

21. There's a rule that says tennis players can't wear camouflage clothes! Tournament officials were worried they wouldn't be able to see the players if they wore camouflage. It's like playing hide and seek and tennis at the same time - not a good combination!

22. One player used to eat grass from the Wimbledon courts when he won! Novak Djokovic started this weird tradition, saying the grass tasted like victory. Other players thought he was crazy - eating tennis court grass is definitely not a normal snack!

23. Some players think it's bad luck to step on the lines between points! They hop or jump over them like they're playing hopscotch. Watch carefully during

matches and you'll see players doing little dances to avoid stepping on lines - it's like the lines are made of hot lava!

24. Tennis players used to carry their rackets in wooden boxes that looked like tiny coffins! These boxes had special compartments for spare strings, balls, and even a mirror to check their hair. Some players would decorate their boxes with stickers, like a tennis-themed treasure chest!

25. The ball kids at some tournaments had to wear white gloves! They thought this made the tournament look fancier, but the kids kept dropping balls because the gloves were slippery. It's like trying to catch soap bubbles while wearing mittens - not very practical!

26. Some tennis courts have been built in really weird places! There's a tennis court on top of a skyscraper in Dubai, one on a cruise ship that moves with the waves,

and even one in an old prison yard. Imagine playing tennis while boats sail by or airplanes fly overhead!

27. Tennis players used to smoke cigarettes during changeovers! Can you believe it? They thought it helped them relax between games. Now we know that's super bad for you, and players drink water and eat bananas instead - much healthier choices!

28. There's a special perfume that smells like tennis balls! Someone actually made a perfume that smells like new tennis balls because lots of people love that smell. It's like wearing the smell of your favorite sport - though you might smell like a tennis bag!

29. Some players think wearing mismatched socks brings good luck! One famous player wore one pink sock and one blue sock in every match. Another player would only wear socks with holes in them because he won an important match while wearing holey socks!

30. The shortest tennis match ever lasted only 20 minutes! One player won so quickly that some fans missed the whole match because they were still buying snacks. The loser was so embarrassed that he pretended he had to catch a train and ran off the court - talk about a quick getaway!

Chapter Eight

Tennis Around the World

Interesting insights into how tennis is celebrated globally, including popular players from different countries.

1. In Australia, kids play tennis before school in the summer! They start super early in the morning because it gets so hot later in the day. Some schools even have special "tennis breakfast clubs" where kids play tennis and then eat breakfast together. It's like having a tennis party every morning before class starts!

2. In Japan, they have tennis courts on top of train stations and shopping malls! Because there isn't much space in big cities like Tokyo, they build tennis courts

on rooftops. Players have to be careful not to hit balls too high, or they might land on the street below! It's like playing tennis in the clouds.

3. Spain has special tennis academies where kids live and learn tennis! Rafael Nadal even started his own academy where children from all over the world come to learn. They go to regular school in the morning and play tennis in the afternoon. It's like going to Hogwarts, but for tennis instead of magic!

4. In India, they play tennis in the mountains! There are tennis courts in the Himalayas at places so high that players sometimes get out of breath just walking to the court. The tennis balls fly differently in the thin air, making the game extra tricky. It's like playing tennis on top of the world!

5. Swiss tennis star Roger Federer started as a ball boy in his hometown tournament! Now kids in Switzerland dream of being ball boys at the same tournament, hop-

ing they'll become tennis stars too. Some Swiss kids even collect Roger Federer stamps because he's so famous that they put his picture on postage stamps!

6. In Brazil, they play beach tennis right next to the ocean! Instead of regular tennis courts, they set up nets on the sand and play with special paddles. Players have to deal with wind, sand, and sometimes even waves that come too close to the court. It's like mixing tennis with a beach party!

7. Chinese schools have "tennis breaks" during the day! Just like we have recess, some schools in China give kids time to play tennis between classes. They believe it helps students concentrate better in class. Imagine having a quick tennis match instead of regular recess - how fun would that be!

8. In Sweden, they play tennis in the middle of winter inside giant heated bubbles! These huge white domes protect the courts from snow and keep players warm

when it's freezing outside. From the outside, they look like giant igloos for tennis! Sometimes the bubbles get so covered in snow that they have to be dug out.

9. South African kids learn to play tennis using walls in townships! They draw court lines on walls and practice hitting balls against them when they don't have real tennis courts. Some of these "wall courts" have become famous, and professional players sometimes visit to play with local kids.

10. Russia has indoor tennis courts that used to be old factories and warehouses! They turned these huge buildings into tennis centers because it's too cold to play outside most of the year. Some still have the old factory windows and high ceilings, making them look like tennis museums!

11. In France, they play tennis in old castles! Some fancy tennis clubs are built in the gardens of historic chateaux (that's French for castles). Players get to walk through

beautiful gardens to reach the courts. It's like being a tennis-playing prince or princess for a day!

12. Argentina has a floating tennis court that moves with the waves! It was built on a lake and bobs up and down as boats pass by. Players have to time their shots with the waves, making it extra challenging. It's like playing tennis on a giant rubber duck in a bathtub!

13. In Croatia, there's a tennis court on top of an ancient Roman arena! Players get to play surrounded by 2,000-year-old walls. Tourists watching matches can sit on the same stone seats that Roman people used long ago. It's like playing tennis in a history museum!

14. British tennis fans at Wimbledon are famous for eating strawberries and cream! They eat about 27,000 kilograms of strawberries during the tournament - that's heavier than four elephants! The strawberries must be picked fresh each morning at 4:00 AM to be ready for that day's matches.

15. In the Netherlands, they have tennis courts that float on canals! When it freezes in winter, these courts turn into ice skating rinks. So players can play tennis in summer and ice skate in winter on the same court. It's like having two sports courts in one!

16. Italian tennis clubs often have pizza ovens right next to the courts! Players can smell fresh pizza while they're playing, and many clubs serve homemade pizza after matches. Some clubs even have special "pizza and play" nights where families eat and play tennis together.

17. In Morocco, they play tennis in the desert! Some courts are surrounded by sand dunes, and players have to clean red desert dust off the courts before matches. Sometimes camels walk past the courts during games, making for a very unusual tennis experience!

18. German tennis clubs have special "midnight tennis" tournaments! Players start matches late at night and play until sunrise, using special lights on the courts. They

drink hot chocolate between matches to stay awake. It's like having a tennis sleepover party!

19. In New Zealand, they have tennis courts next to active volcanoes! Players can sometimes feel the ground rumble during matches, and some courts have special "volcano warnings" posted nearby. It's like playing tennis on a sleeping giant!

20. Canadian tennis players practice in special indoor "bubble" courts during winter! These courts are kept warm while it's snowing outside. Sometimes the bubbles get so covered in snow that they look like giant marshmallows from the outside!

21. In Thailand, they have floating tennis courts on the ocean! Players have to take a boat to reach the court, and if they hit the ball too far, it splashes into the sea. Special ball boys use kayaks to collect balls that go into the water - it's like combining tennis with a boat ride!

22. Greek tennis clubs often build courts among ancient ruins! Players might find old pottery pieces near the courts, and some clubs have special rules about what to do if they discover ancient artifacts while fixing the courts. It's like playing tennis in an archaeology site!

23. In South Korea, they have tennis courts in underground shopping malls! Because space is limited in big cities, they build courts below ground. Players take escalators down to reach the courts, and some even have special viewing windows where shoppers can watch matches while shopping!

24. Mexican tennis clubs often have courts with amazing views of pyramids! Some clubs are built near ancient Mayan ruins, so players can see incredible historical sites while playing. Sometimes iguanas run across the courts during matches - they're like prehistoric ball boys!

25. In Dubai, they built a tennis court on top of a skyscraper! It's so high up that players can see the whole city

while playing. They have to use special nets that won't blow away in the strong winds, and they can only use bright orange balls because regular yellow ones are hard to see against the clouds!

26. Indonesian tennis courts are sometimes built in the middle of rice fields! Players have to walk through rice paddies to reach the courts, and they might see farmers working while they play. During harvest season, the courts are surrounded by golden rice plants - it's like playing in a golden stadium!

27. In Ireland, they paint tennis courts with special paint that helps rain water drain away quickly! Because it rains so much there, they had to figure out how to play tennis even when it's wet. Some courts even have tiny holes in them to help the water disappear faster - like having thousands of tiny drains!

28. Chilean tennis courts in the Andes Mountains are the highest tennis courts in the world! The air is so thin

up there that tennis balls fly much faster and farther than normal. Players have to use special pressurized balls that won't explode in the high altitude - regular balls would pop like balloons!

29. In Poland, they have underground tennis courts in old salt mines! Players take elevators deep underground to reach courts built in huge caves. The walls are made of salt, and players say the air is super clean and good for their health. It's like playing tennis inside a giant salt shaker!

30. African tennis programs often use termite mounds to make court surfaces! They crush up the special dirt that termites use to build their homes because it makes perfect tennis court clay. The termites do all the hard work of finding and processing the perfect dirt - they're like tiny construction workers helping build tennis courts!

Chapter Nine

Junior Tennis and Youth Stars

Stories about young prodigies and how kids get started in competitive tennis.

1. Coco Gauff started playing tennis when she was just 6 years old, and by age 15, she beat her hero Venus Williams at Wimbledon! She was still doing homework between matches and taking school tests online during tournaments. Imagine beating one of the world's best players and then having to finish your math homework!

2. The youngest player to ever win a professional tennis match was Michael Chang at 15 years and 6 months old! He was so young that his parents had to drive him to tournaments because he didn't have a driver's license yet. He drank chocolate milk during matches instead of sports drinks because that's what his mom packed for him!

3. Junior tennis players have special colored balls to help them learn! Red balls are bigger and softer for beginners, orange balls are a bit faster for improving players, and green balls are almost like regular balls. It's like having training wheels on a bike, but for tennis! The courts are smaller too, so kids don't have to run as far.

4. Tracy Austin won a professional tournament when she was 14, wearing braces and pigtails! She was so young that she had to get permission from her teachers to miss school for tournaments. Sometimes she would practice her serves in her backyard before going to school in the morning, still wearing her pajamas!

5. Junior tennis players start learning to keep score using pictures instead of numbers! They use smiley faces, stars, or animals to count points because it's more fun than saying "15-love." Some kids even make up their own scoring systems - like using dinosaurs instead of numbers!

6. Boris Becker won Wimbledon when he was just 17! He was so young that he still had a curfew at home, even though he was a Wimbledon champion. His parents made him clean his room and do his chores even after he became famous. Imagine being the best tennis player in the world but still having to make your bed!

7. Many young tennis players practice hitting balls against garage doors! Roger Federer, Serena Williams, and many other champions started this way. Some garage doors still have marks from where kids hit thousands of tennis balls. It's like having a practice partner that never gets tired!

8. In tennis academies, kids wake up super early to practice before school! They might start hitting balls at 6:00 AM while other kids are still sleeping. After school, they practice again until dinner time. Some academies even have special tennis homework - like watching videos of good tennis shots!

9. Young players in training sometimes use special light-up tennis balls! These balls glow in different colors to show if you're hitting them correctly. Green means perfect, yellow means okay, and red means try again. It's like having traffic lights telling you how well you're playing!

10. Some junior tennis players travel to more than 20 countries before they turn 18! They play in tournaments all over the world and make friends with kids who speak different languages. Many learn to say "good shot" and "good match" in lots of different languages!

11. Andre Agassi's dad made him practice hitting 2,500 balls every single day when he was little! He used a special ball machine nicknamed "the dragon" that would shoot tennis balls at young Andre. By age 12, Andre had hit over a million tennis balls - that's more balls than there are people in some cities!

12. Junior tennis players have special rules about racket sizes! Little kids start with tiny rackets that are perfect for their height. As they grow taller, they get bigger rackets. It's like having a racket that grows with you! Some kids decorate their rackets with stickers to make them more fun.

13. Maria Sharapova moved from Russia to America when she was just 7 years old to train in tennis! She barely spoke English and had to leave her mom behind because they couldn't afford two plane tickets. She practiced tennis all day and learned English by watching cartoons on TV!

14. Some tennis academies have special robots that shoot balls for kids to practice with! These robots can be programmed to hit balls just like famous players. Want to practice returning serves like Serena Williams? The robot can do that! It's like having a mechanical tennis champion as your practice partner.

15. Young tennis players often use colored tape on their rackets to show them where to hit the ball! Green tape means "hit here for good shots," red tape means "try not to hit here." It's like having a tiny tennis coach right on your racket telling you what to do!

16. Martina Hingis started playing tennis before she could walk properly! Her mom was a tennis coach and put a tiny racket in her crib. She won her first tournament at age 4, and by 12, she was winning against grown-ups. She was named after tennis champion Martina Navratilova - talk about being born to play tennis!

17. Junior tennis players have special tournaments called "Tennis Futures"! These are like mini versions of professional tournaments. Kids get to feel like pros, with umpires, ball kids, and sometimes even small crowds watching. Some tournaments even give out tiny trophies that look just like the big ones!

18. Some kids practice tennis wearing special glasses that block their vision when they look down! This helps them keep their eyes on the ball instead of looking at their feet. It's like wearing magic glasses that only let you see tennis balls!

19. The youngest player to ever compete at Wimbledon was Jennifer Capriati at 14 years and 90 days old! She was so young that she had to do her summer reading homework between matches. Tournament officials had to make special passes for her parents because they didn't have rules for players that young!

20. Tennis academies have special "homework courts" where kids can practice and do schoolwork at the same time! They have desks right next to the courts so students can hit balls for a while, then work on their math problems. It's like having a classroom and a tennis court mixed together!

21. Young players learn to serve by practicing with balloons! The slow movement of the balloon helps them learn the right serving motion. Some coaches even draw faces on the balloons to make it more fun. It's like playing tennis in slow motion!

22. Pete Sampras started playing tennis with a racket his parents found at a garage sale for $6! He used to hit balls against his family's refrigerator until they finally built a wall in their backyard for him to practice against. Now kids can buy rackets that cost hundreds of dollars!

23. Some junior tennis programs have "tennis libraries" where kids can borrow different rackets to try! Just like

borrowing books from a regular library, they can test different rackets to find the one they like best. They even get a special tennis library card!

24. Young tennis players often practice with foam balls indoors! These soft balls don't break windows or knock things over, so kids can practice anywhere. Some kids even practice in their bedrooms before going to sleep - just don't tell mom!

25. Tennis academies have special "mistake courts" where kids are only allowed to try crazy shots! The rule is that you have to try something new, even if you miss. It helps players learn new skills without being afraid of making mistakes. It's like having permission to be silly with tennis!

26. Some junior tennis players have special diaries where they draw pictures of their best shots! They use different colors for different shots - red for serves, blue for

backhands, green for forehands. It's like making a comic book about your tennis adventures!

27. In some countries, kids start playing tennis with wooden paddles before using real rackets! This helps them learn to control their shots without the ball going too fast. The paddles make a fun "pop" sound when they hit the ball - like playing ping pong but bigger!

28. Junior tennis players learn to count games by collecting colorful wristbands! Every time they win a game, they get to put on another band. By the end of the match, some kids look like they're wearing rainbow bracelets up their arms!

29. Some tennis academies have courts with special lines that light up! The lights show kids where to run and where to stand for different shots. It's like having a giant video game court that teaches you how to play tennis!

30. Young tennis players often name their tennis rackets! Some kids give their rackets superhero names because

they think it gives them special powers on the court. One young player called her racket "Wonder Woman" and would talk to it during matches for good luck!

Chapter Ten

Tennis for Everyone

A look at wheelchair tennis, adapted forms of the game, and how everyone can enjoy tennis regardless of ability level.

1. In wheelchair tennis, players can let the ball bounce twice instead of just once! The first bounce must be in the court, but the second bounce can be anywhere. This makes for super exciting rallies that last longer than regular tennis matches. Some players are so good they usually only need one bounce anyway!

2. Esther Vergeer is one of the most amazing tennis players ever - she won 470 matches in a row in wheelchair

tennis! That's more wins than any other tennis player in history. She didn't lose a single match for ten whole years. Even the greatest players like Roger Federer and Serena Williams never had a winning streak that long!

3. Blind tennis players use special balls that make jingling sounds! These balls have little bells inside them so players can hear where the ball is going. The courts also have different textures on the ground to help players know where they are. It's like playing tennis using your ears instead of your eyes!

4. Some tennis players use special chairs that can spin super fast! These sports wheelchairs are like race cars - they can turn quickly and move really fast across the court. They have angled wheels and special bars on the back to help players make sharp turns, like a tennis version of a Ferrari!

5. Walking tennis is perfect for people who want to play slower! Players aren't allowed to run - they have to walk

to hit the ball. This makes the game more relaxing and fun for people who don't want to sprint around. It's like playing tennis in slow motion!

6. The Paralympics tennis matches are just as exciting as regular tennis! Players hit the ball just as hard and make amazing shots. Sometimes the rallies are even longer because the special tennis chairs can move so quickly around the court. Many people say these matches are more fun to watch!

7. Tennis courts can have special bumpy lines to help blind players feel where they are! The lines are raised up like tiny speed bumps, so players can feel them with their feet or wheelchair. Some courts even have different textures for different areas, like a giant touch-and-feel book!

8. Beach tennis is great for everyone because the soft sand is easier on your legs! Players can dive for balls without getting hurt because they land in fluffy sand.

It's like playing tennis on a giant cushion! Plus, if you get too hot, you can jump in the ocean to cool off.

9. Some tennis programs use balloons instead of tennis balls for beginners! This makes the game slower and gives players more time to hit the ball. The balloons float in the air longer, so nobody has to rush. It's like playing tennis with a friendly cloud!

10. Unified tennis pairs players with and without disabilities on the same team! They play doubles together and learn from each other. It's a great way to make new friends and show that everyone can enjoy tennis together. Some pairs become such good friends that they practice together every week!

11. Short tennis uses smaller courts and softer balls! This makes it perfect for anyone just starting out or people who want to play in a smaller space. You can even set up a short tennis court in your driveway or playground. It's like having a mini tennis playground anywhere you go!

12. Sound tennis has special beeping lines around the court! These lines make different noises to help blind players know where they are on the court. The net makes a different sound too, so players know when they're getting close. It's like having a musical tennis court!

13. Some wheelchair tennis players can hit serves faster than 100 miles per hour! That's faster than most cars are allowed to drive on the highway. They use their strong arms and special spinning techniques to hit the ball super fast. The chairs are designed not to tip over even when hitting such powerful shots!

14. Tennis clubs have started making "sensory-friendly" courts! These courts have quieter areas, softer lights, and less busy backgrounds to help players who get overwhelmed by too much noise and movement. It's like having a calm, peaceful tennis bubble where everyone can feel comfortable!

15. Cardio tennis is for people who just want to have fun and exercise! There's no scoring or winning - players just hit balls and move around to music. It's like having a tennis dance party! Some classes even use glow-in-the-dark balls when playing in the evening.

16. Special tennis rackets exist that are lighter and easier to hold! Some have bigger handles, some have shorter handles, and some even have two handles. These rackets are designed so everyone can find one that feels just right for them. It's like Goldilocks finding the perfect tennis racket!

17. Table tennis is a great way for everyone to enjoy tennis-style games! You can play sitting down, and the table can be adjusted to different heights. Some tables even have special sides that fold up to return the ball if you want to practice alone. It's like having a robot practice partner!

18. Family tennis has special rules where everyone gets to play together! Parents and kids use different sized courts on the same tennis court, so nobody has an unfair advantage. Grandparents can play too - some families have three generations playing together! It's like having a tennis party with your whole family.

19. Some tennis programs use velcro walls and balls! The balls stick to special patches on the wall, making it easier to hit targets. This helps players practice their aim and have fun at the same time. It's like playing darts with tennis balls!

20. Wheelchair tennis players sometimes do amazing tricks! They can spin their chairs in complete circles while hitting the ball, and some can even pop wheelies between points. It's like watching a tennis circus performance! Some players say spinning in their chair helps them hit better shots.

21. Tennis courts can have special markings for different games! One court might have lines for regular tennis, short tennis, and wheelchair tennis all at once. The lines are painted in different colors so players don't get confused. It's like having three tennis courts in one!

22. Some programs use tennis balls attached to elastic strings! The ball bounces back to you after each hit, so you don't have to chase it. This is great for players who want to practice alone or have trouble moving around the court. It's like having a tennis ball on a yo-yo!

23. Touch tennis uses foam balls that move super slowly through the air! This gives players more time to reach the ball and hit it back. The foam balls don't hurt if they hit you, so players feel more confident trying to hit hard shots. It's like playing tennis with marshmallows!

24. Special tennis nets can be set up at any height! Some players use lower nets when they're starting out, and the nets can be raised as players improve. You can even

string a net between two chairs to play mini-tennis in your living room! It's like having an adjustable tennis playground.

25. Beach wheelchair tennis has special chairs with big, wide wheels! These wheels don't sink into the sand, so players can move around easily on the beach. Some chairs even float in water, so players can cool off between games! It's like having a tennis-playing dune buggy.

26. Social tennis clubs focus on making friends rather than winning! Everyone plays with different partners, and between games, players share snacks and stories. Some clubs have special signals you can use if you want to take a break and just chat. It's like having a tennis tea party!

27. Tennis robots can be adjusted to throw balls at any speed! This means players can practice at whatever pace feels comfortable for them. Some robots can even re-

member your favorite practice patterns. It's like having a personal tennis coach that never gets tired!

28. Some programs use giant tennis balls that are as big as beach balls! These are great for players who are just starting out or have trouble seeing regular tennis balls. They move slowly through the air and are easy to hit. It's like playing tennis with the moon!

29. Tennis courts can have special cushioned surfaces! These surfaces are easier on players' bodies and wheelchairs. They're bouncy like a trampoline but not too bouncy - just right for playing tennis comfortably. It's like playing tennis on a giant pillow!

30. Sitting tennis is played by players sitting on the ground or in regular chairs! The court is smaller, and the net is lower, but the fun is just as big. Some players say they can hit better shots sitting down because they don't have to worry about running around. It's like playing tennis in your favorite comfy chair!

31. Red Ball Tennis is perfect for anyone learning the game! The red balls are bigger, softer, and bounce 75% slower than regular tennis balls. They even have special red ball tournaments where everyone plays with these slower balls. The courts are smaller too - about the size of a large bathroom! It's like playing tennis in slow-motion while you learn the game. Even some professional players practice with red balls when they're learning new shots!

Printed in Great Britain
by Amazon